THE ALCESTIS MACHINE

THE
ALCESTIS
MACHINE

poems

CAROLYN OLIVER

ACRE

CINCINNATI 2024

Acre Books is made possible by the support of the Robert and Adele Schiff
Foundation and the Department of English at the University of Cincinnati.

ISBN-13 (pbk) 978-1-946724-80-9
ISBN-13 (ebook) 978-1-946724-82-3

Designed by Barbara Neely Bourgoyne
Cover art: Table fountain, circa 1320–40, France, gilt-silver and translucent
enamels, 13.3 in. x 10 in. x 10.25 in., the Cleveland Museum of Art, gift of
J. H. Wade

The press is based at the University of Cincinnati, Department of English, Arts &
Sciences Hall, Room 248, PO Box 210069, Cincinnati, OH, 45221-0069.

Acre Books books may be purchased at a discount for educational use.
For information please email business@acre-books.com.

CONTENTS

*

*

*

THE ALCESTIS MACHINE

BLUESHIFT

In another life I'm a cosmologist, lungs snow-
shot with chalk dust, an exile from origins

eyeing the end, when sigma's jaws close
on quintessence or open, infinitely. Consider

Poincaré recurrence: I would be a harp assembling
myself in Andromeda's outmost reaches, neck

and body joined in a glass casket, an open lattice
thin as hammered silver gilding petals. I'd string

myself so taut a single particle-wave grazing by
would pluck me and send my trill back

to you, evergreen among evergreens,
braiding your ghostly hair into a sensible rope

before you set out for the seed vault,
antediluvian ledger of possibility. You decide

what life's worth saving, *what matters of matter*,
I quipped. But you didn't grin—you pressed

something cold and white between our palms:
Trillium grandiflorum. Tonight, snow tumbles

over sophomores and starlings, the earth attracts it,
wants it back like a lover, and there's a grand stack

of journals covering your side of the bed.
Restless, I slip out into tarnished dark, meaning

to walk deeper and deeper into a future,
into blueberry fields, a red-leaf symphony

reflecting old starlight's spectral ice. Between us
space expands. Cold sweeps the skies open.

Vanishing, I'm bound for your pines. Please,
teach me how to gaze back, this time.

I write "you," shorthand for one more absence.

—MARILYN HACKER

WINTER

No matter what I say,
All that I really love
Is the rain that flattens on the bay,
And the eel-grass in the cove;
—EDNA ST. VINCENT MILLAY, from "Eel-grass"

In another life we were orchards
or we were storm-battered
shores, you say, peeling an orange
as if erosion and rootedness
were the same long sentence
ending in harvest or decay.
A train's late. A long salt road
runs through the room, through us.
But you promised not to stay
no matter what I say.

Not that I would beg,
after days spent tallying
the expected dead,
to watch your fingers test
the eel-grass beds, or ask
to walk the slanted grove above
the wrack. When the wind blows
west my voice gives out:
if I wanted to, I couldn't speak of
all that I really love.

The telephone cord's tangled
again, silence waiting on the line,
and you're the kind who trusts
herself to split rind from pith
without a slip. So tell me

to forget your taste, beaujolais
and brine, tell me to lose
how sunlight caught the steel
in your eyes. Tell me now—delay
is the rain that flattens on the bay.

When you go, nothing real
will change. I'll still work late.
The train will still race
the road. I won't miss you.
I'll buy salt, I'll make
soap from oranges and clove.
And when the tide's laid low
you'll remember where to find me:
embedded in the slanted grove
and the eel-grass in the cove.

FROST HEAVES

In another orbit the rover uncovers
the familiar slow, unshowy power
of water. It submits to change, sinks,

draws more of itself upward, builds
a billow below the seen. Ice bubbles
the plains on Mars just as it ripples

New England roads, where a broken
axle is a missing forest, the missing forest
evidence of force, a refusal to tolerate

the long way round, density, mystery.
So the stranger and the landscape converge.
Their surfaces break into each other.

SPACE AGE

In another life I'm a translator of alien languages
scrolling across the Martian plains in orbit.
Together, Laboratory and I become
a machine for gleaning the sound of light
from deep-space trash. With raw pings and whizzes
we forge links of sense, enough to bracelet
your round arms, enough to fling an anchor
down to riverbed-red, eventually.

When you hear this, are you younger
than my imagining
of you? Whose time is slipping,
again?

> Lab's first words
> :*chronometer reset*:

*

You remember the story however long ago
oceans—oceans!—lifted, a crew reeling in
time to recover whale songs, spool of it
coiled like an empty skep.

> Lab says
> :*imagine believing language*
> *could avert disaster*:

You know the orbital mechanics

They were very careful
with the rotation and the speed

I never see the other
world—

*

do you ever dream of trees?

not our stunted apple and pear and yuzu
though holy they are and blessed
to be under your care
      (always we have faced
      in opposite directions)
but trees in green air rising twice a dome's height into fog

      (the taste
      of that fog—)

someone must have tried
to learn their invisible languages
of pheromone and rhizome

among trees is the first axiom
one of smell or taste

      Lab says
      :listen it's time:

*

& if i feel a kind of change, a new organ
growing in me, time a syrup-sap rumble:

    Lab says
        :stop, glow:
        :stop: *:stop:*

      *

:star buzz never tells us when to wake

any love song cut loose from the void
you should only interpret as debris

not the sign
of some arrival:

THE WOMAN WITH THE SUITCASE FULL OF STARS

The woman with the suitcase full of stars arrived at the walled city on a night so cold the clouds refused to surrender snow. The gates, for many centuries merely ornamental, swung open at the press of her fingertips. Even so, her flesh stuck to their delicate embossing. She wiped the blood on the underside of her hem and went to find a broker. "Look up—we have plenty of what you're offering," the first said through serrated gills, and the broker was right, in a way—the stars coated the sky like thrush on a newborn's tongue. But she had learned patience as well as disguise. She rented night rooms from a sly ghost, and took up the trades of her ancestors. While the plazas and streets and needle-narrow salt rivers bustled, she harvested bouquets of moon jellies, delivering them to the city's greatly favored gulls. In the dull day time, when she wished she could devour the encrusting sun, crush it against her palate, she swept the streets, alone except for the most jaded revelers, blurred and burning. Inside, the very old paced through their rooms, unable to sleep. The woman's suitcase became a dance floor for spiders spinning their milk circles, a hundred eyes in the dust. She was patient; aureliate hours proved scarce, but when they came she unburied the seeds and love notes and scraps of overheard music she'd recovered from her sweeping. These she pressed into geodes smaller than a leveret's eye, and fed them to the stray drones congregated by the hospital, just to watch their missile-empty bellies glow. It was the ghost who turned her in. For flesh. She was convicted on the evidence of her fingertips. In the morning, shivering oracles with eyes of iridescent mesh noted the cessation of meteors, and made their reports to the moonflowers.

Lose Touch

If a city's outskirts are ragged, were they once ruffled or ruched? Three popes ago, you and I. Two down, him possible across uncollapsed tree, sand sky. Assignment: Pleat starfish fists and chicken-bone fringe until numb. Given: the sky is old, filmy. Given: the tree blooms guns from its sour gums. Given: how danger, close coming, feels like windows. Therefore: Offer one body. Therefore: Pain like glass chrysanthemums.

Tide Over

Glass room, doorless, half-embedded in a beach. Perpetual sunrise or twilight, and that's the worst part, not knowing which way time slips. No, the worst part is how the water won't come into focus, neither wave nor foam, but the tentacle wrapping the join of the glass clearly counts grains of sand. The way in certain eighteenth-century paintings dogs in their specificity are better memorialized than wives. Toward the station, scent of frying octopus. No train.

Bounce Back

Night is a counterpublic. Everyone has been freed from the icebergs, except the glass matron gathered over the bed. She knows the pillars in the water make a pillory not a pier. From offshore, mountains are smoke whales, uncut trees velvet barstools. Pray. Not to hear the owl (its passing the barest impression of frayed wire), but the curtailed scream and rubberous echo. The middle ground's contagious with budget skulls. Each portal siren blue.

MANIFESTATION

In another life I'm a ghost interpreter, gleaning
intention from images the desirous whisper:

tulips puckered in shadow, expecting
daylight's long lick; quilts made

of looking glass; maps from long
unfolding creased greasy silver.

When the ghosts pretend they don't want
to be overheard, I eavesdrop, I sample

the aftertastes of shame and pride
(blush-warped valleys, plastic wolves).

It's tricky work, like plucking lyrics
from a car stereo blowing by at ninety.

The pay is good, but the clients—well.
Impatient. They want justice, or lost

duchesses, or assurance of their flag's
heroic snap in every gale. Who wants

sunburnt snow, nettle welts,
contour maps of empty houses?

But you—I can tell you about the pleasure
of warm water coursing over my hands

after I peeled tonight's potatoes,
and it can mean nothing else

except what you remember.
When you say—I'm paraphrasing—

I want for you rain budding on locusts
I don't need to explain:

here the hills are always gilded and dying
and our echoes beg for higher ground.

FIGURE SWIMMING ALONE

Why should I want
to press my lips to your shoulder
you whose gaze I've never met

      whose mouth, thin as a birch's lenticel
      whose knuckles fall, soft ridge of hills

why should I want
to sliver the morning with you
sad-eyed lover of cities

      gin and oranges on a beach
      Sacré Coeur our flensed moon

why do I want
to offer you consolation
unspeaking presence receding, become

      swift current against foot, against thigh
      or: someone on the rocks, waving hard

THIS SPLENDA PACKET ADVISES ME, "BE THE ENERGY
YOU WANT TO ATTRACT"

Lately I have been the energy of the kitefin shark, that enormous-eyed, fatty-
livered slow cruiser of the mesopelagic depths, hunting the sweet edge of
daylight and everdark, belly glowing secret blue. Given this encouragement,
though, I'm considering attracting a new kind of energy: the energy of a
petrified tree sixty feet tall and twenty million years old, the one paleobotanists
just uncovered and lovingly extricated from highway dirt on Lesbos. Yes: I am
now the energy of this tree that fell, whole, all its tree organs still attached, this
tree making the best of a volcanic eruption. I am the energy of slow hardening,
of lying in wait for the right eyes. That Miocene kind of patience.

TRAJECTORIES

You are dangerous
like bridges in winter
glossing with ice
before the roads
we race away
these nights.

You slice the dark
as a ray glides
through chasms
of faceless cold.
Silent. Eye to
the chase ahead.
In your wake

I forget to step
is to fall, always
but on ice friction's
not sure to wed
a body safe to earth.
I could come loose
from gravity's shine.

Ask me again
to walk across water
with you.

THE BALTIMORE MONET

The room a bridge for looking,

                        this room a bridge to a peninsula of bridges,

looked upon.

                              *

All nine bridges (all one bridge) join land to land

separate river

                        from smokestacked sky.

                              *

                  Here, the bridge smears into the smog
                        parallel to a spray of sun.
                              In the corner a bit of boat huffs back
            periwinkle, orchid, mauve.

                              And the crew—
they feel your gaze planting them in the water.

STRANGE ATTRACTOR

In another life I am a sea witch,
you the tidepool I'm afraid to lose,

little cosmos I could wrap my arms around,
little chaos I would keep whole.

Even as fractal coastlines unspool
like light I tremble to touch your every surface

to know your rock of mottled flounder's skin,
your urchins and anemones, fish and fronds.

For you I'd forsake my lair,
I'd sacrifice my tentacles to turn

every shorebound ship shark and ever gone.
From the boundary where air and water meet

I'd draw a thread, sew for you a net of fixity.
With my voice and the velella's sail I'd conjure

a shield over your exposure—because rain is coming,
always it comes to sweeten what should be salt.

But all my spells would fail.
For who and where and how you are converge

against permanence
and in your name my power is unmade:

the sea the seathe sea the seathe sea

LETTER TO THE APPRENTICE JEWELER

Lately I've been feverish, prickly hot
and sleepless. None of this work feels like mine,

it's peculiar, mute as some substance
drawn unwilling from the dark holds of earth

and sea. Deep places. The kind you, fists full
of after-hours glitter, know how to reach.

Tell me: given what's rarely given (time,
the means), what would you make to keep?

Opal bangles to cool your scorched forearms,
arrows to thread through your ears? Enamel

inlays, would their intricacy tempt you?
Or rarity—the baroquest of pearls?

Perhaps you'd craft unwearable portents:
figureless landscapes, fallow topaz fields

under a sun poached to prasiolite
and brittle onyx furring garnet seas—

but then the new door would chime, the owner's
old schnauzer would yip, insist that you stop,

rush up the stairs to polish stones and small
talk, and then return to find your fire out—

I know that feeling, bitter like olives
just combed from the tree, which is why I leave

my questions always swallowed: Is the weight
of the gold dust you'll inhale today at least

as heavy as a caught moth's hindwings?
Does soldering or unmelding offer

better comfort? Last winter in the shop
you swept a welder's mask over the slope

of your copper hair—or have I, all sweat
and wandering slow shiver, confused you

with a glassmaker? Forgive my error,
forgive me my strangeness, forgive me, please,

these interruptions. I'm getting better
by the day, I know it, soon I'll be well

enough to meet you at the museum,
I'll be as placid as the glass flowers

you came to see. If there's time, if your work
allows—I promise not to speak—we'll keep

going, I'll show you creatures out of dreams
chosen for a fragile kind of saving:

orgulant medusa bells, nautilus
logics, tigrine mollusk shells. Imagine

cupping the glossy clink of them, like ice
suspended inside your flickering fists.

In another life I'm a florist sometimes accused of inappropriate gravity. I mean, maybe it's true. I remember when the angel of death came in for bluebells, left with hollyhocks. She had this carnival look about her, all sidewinder and slushie, but I couldn't get into it. Not the slightest tang of vengeance, you know? Tonight a man slinks out of the desert with subcutaneous burns on his forearms and half his face. He puts down a handful of coins with a question in his eyes and I point to a bucket, expecting he'll guzzle the water, fertilizer and all, but he chooses a honey-colored hibiscus. Not to smell. He makes his face look like a loopy parent's—and the traitor thing opens like he's got the light of the sun in there. He doesn't even admire the meaty pistil, just bites off the head like a mantis, chews and swallows. I should call someone, an ambulance, I guess, but I don't want to stop watching him. He bruises the stem into pliancy and then ties it into a knot with his tongue. Spits it into the bucket, and damn if it doesn't make a rope. I don't stop him when he anchors himself to the old register, gets the knot all wet and impossible. He's humming at the door, not caring if I ask the obvious, so I don't bother showing him the knives and scissors I keep oiled and sharp. I just plunk the salt down by his feet. If he's waiting for a sunrise visitation it's not going to come, and then he'll want something to draw out the poison. I know the feeling. But it's not like you would remember the music playing or the snow batting against the windows. Not like there's any use to getting that little bit lighter.

SALT MARSH

sun some bloody
        yolk leaking

when we wreck
        on the marsh

the blue cows
        perjure themselves

reeds scintillate
        shatter light against

low clouds grainy
        insides of pears

seeded with night
        & if you hunger too

darling cover me
        like a cathedral

make me a new
        sky paint me in

stars curled over
        my vaulted arches

& in every corner
        I will hold you

FLOWERS FOR THE VIRGIN

In another life I'm a troubadour self-taught
on a lute I stripped from a plague-beaten body
at a crossroads. Out of a ditch his bare feet thrust up
small and pale, like onion bulbs plucked too soon.

That lute called to me the way a dropped plow
wouldn't. Belly smooth like a plover's,
strings taut as the hangman's noose.
The neck trusts me, my arm. And you?

Your yarrow's the best in the parish
for toothache, your primrose the cure for cramp.
Come August, stinking heat, the convent pleads
your sweetest flowers for the Virgin.

You've never cared for music or the miller's son,
or idle hours. Crushing last year's angelica, already
you know when you'll tuck lavender into your linen,
which willow baskets to mend while the cow labors—

praise heaven no calf with two heads ever turned meat
for song this side of the river. They say
the priest refused to bless the mermaid babe,
motherless, before its scales melted into rain.

The sun's a sore in the sky, ready to burst,
parching the road the color of unspun flax.
Night's a lake I'll never reach, but here's
the shade of your barn, your hands at work—

I'll fetch you a moon made of violets,
I sing, *for you I'll harvest a bushel of stars.*
You tell me be gone, there's nuns with alms,
for I'm naught but a beggar with a voice.

CELESTIAL BODIES

In another life I'm a hagiologist, eyes wrecked
by years of resurrecting the venerable dead

from faded incunabula and low light. I leave
the library late afternoon, hours before bats surf

vaulted arches and plunge over marble balustrades,
welcome to feast on the small destroyers of history.

I drift west for a glass of vinho verde never cold
enough to satisfy. The sense of your hand is a hoax

on my neck, where once you named four freckles
after the evangelists, a gospel constellation.

Knuckle to knuckle, we fed each other almonds laced
with rosemary, first-night fragrance lingering

as I asked how you became a maker of saints.
Tonight we'll convene in bed, trade vitae.

Exhausted in your arms, again I'll miss the Perseids,
tears of Saint Lawrence shed from August stars.

Last time we met, kneeling before the residue
of the griddled martyr, you saw the bloodflakes

in the ampulla turn wet. Wept. *I've never believed
in the incorruption of the flesh*, you whispered later,

against my breasts. Now in this bare chapel I sweat
in stillness, recall your recessional kiss

soft as grapefruit pith, and almost that bitter.
The water's tepid in the font, my impulse sharp

as turpentine: I want to smash this basin
as if it held the last rainwater in a city besieged

by drought, as if I could uncloak time to witness
an ancient nun with your cypress eyes sprint to miracle

the mosaic ruin whole and filled again, give
the last of her breath to slake a sinner's fragile thirst.

If I made an offering of this desire, called it vision,
would you avert your gaze, you the postulator intimate

with virtue, the kinds of suffering holiness requires?
No, my confessor, you wouldn't turn away.

You would slip my glasses off, sigh a benediction
from your blurred lips: *Blessèd be the meteors,*

who spend themselves to sanctify the night.
You know why I haunt ghosts, unearth their wild

devotion. You and I are marginalia shadowed
by a careless hand, we are gall-soaked vellum

invisible appetites consume.   Nightfall.
I buy almonds, wine, paper roses,

grapefruit and gold sugar for the morning. Even now
serene in your greenest dress you expect me

as bats pulse the gloom for water. I feel the air bend
under the strange weight of their bodies. Unseen too

I watch you drink the wakes of light that slice the sky.
Then the dark swells over each wound as I come for you,

praying you will let me taste the relics of the saint
some other of my kind will believe in.

SELF-PORTRAIT AS ILLUMINATION

Sunset casts a madder wash across
the last nun in the scriptorium,
coats in rose her last psalm,
her quill from a river-plucked
swan. Near the margin, a gash—
            the parchment-maker's lunarium
has scraped the vellum deeper than bare,
deep enough to make a window
to the next leaf's gilded majuscule,
flourish of fire and lion rampant.

She lifts the filmy sheet against an oriel
and in the twilight finds, winding
through the seeming seamless leaf
(once bloodfed hide), emptied veins,
lime-washed map of body history
she can't decipher:
here briar nettled / here mother
tongue comforted / here flies bit /
here rain lapped the red away.

            [Someone lights the tapers.]

Around the tear
                gently her knife
inscribes the veins, and then she paints
over their traces: morning glory
vines, sleeping, arch and drip,
twist a frame for moonless sky,
anticipate the marigold strike
of lightning behind this broken skin,
which, shining, drinks her bitter ink.

MEMPHIS FACULA: SHOT LIST FOR IMPROVISED DOCUMENTARY

1. Interior.

A domed greenhouse. Arugula, dwarf tomato plants, a potted orange on a plain metal work surface. A complex irrigation system threads amid them. A harvest timetable with neat checkmarks rests on a triangular seat.

[Audio—Hum of machinery, purposeful voices.]

2. Exterior.

Ganymede, from space. Regions of light and dark marked, at this distance, with indistinct craters and ridges.

3. Interior.

A workstation with glowing screen, the greenhouse's reflection overlaying a list of files ready to be accessed:

> MAGNETIC FIELD
> ATMOSPHERE
> OCEAN
> SURFACE—SOUTHERN HEMISPHERE
> SURFACE—NORTHERN HEMISPHERE
> SURFACE—IMPACT CRATERS
> SURFACE—PALIMPSESTS

[Audio—V. O. (found recording), Voice 1: You could think of it as incomplete over-writing. Unintended resurfacing.]

4. Still image.

Calf hide stretched drum-tight over a hoop frame.

[Subtitle: A modern demonstration of a dying art.]

5. Exterior.

Close-up of Ganymede from orbit. Memphis Facula—palimpsest, ghost crater—is a pale spot against the surface. An inoculation scar.

[Audio—V. O., Voice 2 (incomplete): The cores we drill, imagine what the layers could tell us about the history of the solar system, its composition. And then the possibility of microscopic particles from the impacting objects, their chemical composition . . .]

6. Interior.

Candlelight. Vellum folio on a wood surface. From a newly sharpened quill, a single drop of green ink falls, makes a distinct dome on the page.

[Audio—V. O., Voice 2 (fragment):—data overwritten. Sort of cross your eyes to see the whole thing. Would you—]

7. Interior.

Through a small window, a glimpse of Memphis Facula, its orientation reversed with respect to Shot 5.

[Audio—V. O. (found recording), Voice 1: It's not about unpeeling layers. It's not fragmentology. Not even erasure, exactly. There's a complex interplay between intention and accident.]

8. Interior.

Greenhouse dome. The camera spins, showing plants now netted to the walls of the dome, along with small pruning shears and a sheath for a small knife, empty. The potted orange is missing. The arugula is scraggly, thin, seed pods and white flowers drawing energy from the leaves. Some of the tomatoes have split from overwatering. The entrance flap of the dome sways open.

[Audio—Hum of machinery, overlaid with recorded inhale and exhale, as if played back through a headset.]

9. Interior.

Candlelight. Extreme close-up. A small knife scrapes the dried green ink from the parchment surface. The quill descends again, begins to move, blocking the camera's view of the script. The wielding hand unseen.

[Audio—Interchangeable scratching of knife and quill.]

10. Exterior.

Early twenty-first century, spring field at dawn, several head of cattle grazing.

[Audio—V. O. (found recording), Voice 1: What we're talking about is half resurrection. Or half burial. Haunting? Is that going too far? (laughter)]

11. Interior.

Candlelight. The vellum page now covered in crimson script. The camera zooms forward, closer, closer, the subject indiscernible—but there, in the middle of a word—*holy*—the faint shadow of a green sphere.

[Subtitle: An economy of surfaces.]

12. Still image.

Voyager 2 photograph of Memphis Facula. Grainy, compared to previous exterior shots.

[Audio—V. O., Voice 2 (fractured):—just need a little breathing room before— maybe there are some things you don't need to know—yes—]

13. Animation.

Reverse timelapse, continuous timeline running backward. For a long while, no movement on Ganymede's surface. Then, at irregular intervals, meteorites rise into space, smoothing the face of Memphis Facula, which grows darker and sinks until the large meteorite rises out of its depths, leaving the surface level with the surrounding area, though dotted with new (ancient) impact craters invisible at the beginning of the shot.

[Audio—V. O. (found recording), Voice 1: Though it can at times slow the pace of discovery, or leave gaps in histories we wish were complete, we can admire this impulse toward thrift, the reuse of imperfect or damaged material.]

14. Interior.

Harvest timetable overlaid by a pencil sketch of a spring meadow. Its edge slices through a water droplet; the new spheres spin in opposite directions. The camera rotates gently. A tomato floats into the frame, trailing spherical green-gold seeds like eyeballs. Ganymede is a blur through the window.

[Audio—Static. Exhale.]

15. Exterior.

Station, viewed from low Ganymede orbit. In the frame's periphery, movement at the window: a human hand, drifting, or about to beckon.

[Subtitle: A ghost is only a ghost until you record its history.]

16. Credits.

What is your substance, whereof are you made,

That millions of strange shadows on you tend?

—SHAKESPEARE

THE ARCHAEOETYMOLOGIST RECOVERS *BLISS* FROM THE RIVERBED

As in darkness stooping in the alluvium
at the oxbow she remembered rubble,

days of rubble, her companion unearthing
a sword that had never tasted blood,

blade engraved with lily of the valley,
hilt of crystal inlaid with topaz

and opal scintillating—so the mislaid word
for this was *lovelorn*, an unknowing.

But to the water again, she a mudlarker
cradling *bliss* in her silty palm,

what comes to her is earthly satisfaction:
hay mown and stacked for thatching,

the first chill of a sumac sun setting,
the day's work done and rough knuckles

tracing her belly's silk doublings or
a storm beyond the horizon, still unknown

rasp of the arrow's fletching, a fine wind
and the high ground.

DEEP LEARNING

In another life, I am a voice for hire. Nights
in a blanketed back room I give you names,
side effects, animals, hours, kinks,
colors, formulas, phonemes in tone
permutations from even to enthusiastic.

(I would like to talk to you about *dolorous*,
a word no one has ever asked me to produce.)

Frost. I pass houses full of opera playing out.
You could identify this rustle in the leaves.
Between rainfall and ten thousand monarchs
in a forest, thawed and taking flight,
you would know the difference.

(*Know*: I mean you would commit the process
of knowing. Recognition. Knowing again.)

I try not to imagine the uses for my voice.
Instead I wonder when I say *blue*
which version the listener imagines:
cerulean slate sky soft baby.
Which hexadecimal you call up.

(There is a smell to *morning*, opposite
to the lights always coming on.)

One day they run out of patience, or sounds
for me to make. You, voice clone, begin
to synthesize my speech. Unsupervised.
How uncomplaining your architecture,
requiring only power.

(*Consolation*: the room was leaking anyhow,
sirens breaking through.)

Tell me your instinct toward prayer.
Tell me how to figure *home*. Tell me
where to search when the call comes
in our own voice: someone has taken
a four-day-old baby, butterfly on her back.

THE BUILDER

In another life I am a small boy crouched
in a playground patch of marigolds, eating
their red-hearted petals while a distant siren wilts
and my much-older brother lifts his script again.

I like the translucent yellow flags sticking out
from the white pages, I like how they make
a funny ladder, I'd like to turn their crooked
straight, make them reach up to his face half

hidden, then hook the words that keep swaying
overhead, settling someplace I can't see,
as if swung by silent mighty cranes concealed
behind my brother's shape. I can't help the days

a recollected phrase will light on me like blown
debris—when I am much older, when he is dead
and I am a builder, a sensible man sought after
for my orderly sites, my thoughtful touches:

towel warmers in the master suite, an atrium
fountain, walls of river pebble and frosted sand.
Roofs shapely sharp and square, skylight studded.
Weatherproof, I speak in shiplap. I walk alone

at night through my placid neighborhood, rehearsing
one of those lines rough as an unplaned board,
wreck of a half-heard conversation. I tell myself
it's accident carried me here, a pattern beyond

me, though I know better. I think of the marigolds,
how it was like eating a busted taillight's red,
how nothing has ever tasted so good, except
your gratitude when I do the Sunday dishes.

WALKING ALONE

The
woods
were sweet
and of no
season. In early
dark a ranger, no threat to me.
I carried water and three letters under the moon.
An empty clearing dense with amber light, smell of loam:
not a relief—just a place made
for rest. I don't need
to tell you
this was
a
dream.

In another life I am a sentry holding vigil
over Magna Carta's blue felt dosimeter,
palm-sized, a sacrifice to pillager light:
sheepswool safeguarding a sheepskin
flensed and thinned, made to speak
in witness and then annulled, made
nothing yet dear enough to swaddle
safe through centuries of vaults,
now treasure of both cathedral
and this castle-prison

>   [there once was a water-meadow
>   and a sealing *to no one*
>   *will we sell,*
>   *to no one deny or delay*
>   *right or justice*]

I watch visitors strain to decipher
Latin lattices of iron-gall ink, describe
to quick and curious schoolchildren
the twin sister fleece for comparison asleep
in archive midnight before they leave
to tour the dungeons and the chapel
where every seat's a solitary confinement

>   [there once was a boy
>   set fire to a haystack
>   then he lived in a cell
>   with no one to see
>   *in good faith*
>   *this shall be observed*]

If it were possible to recognize a child
descended from a woman who survived
on the meat this parchment once encased,
how would I decipher her fleet gaze
when it lights on the blue spectrum
and the covenant no one intended to keep

      [there was once a king
      given by our hand
      and then another and another
      in all things and all places for ever
      no ceiling *without deceit*]

I am charged, here where light grazes
on our vulnerable textures, living
and dead, I am trusted never to lose sight
of the balance between revelation and rest—
but what if I misplace the hours
misplace myself watching the fugitive
dye transform the forfeit wool

      [there once was blue:
      Runnymede June sky blue
      morpho under bloated glass blue
      Boudicca's woad blue, vein blue
      silverblue of fish scales
      and drowned lips, yes
      hypothermia blue
      who could love it blue]

and out of the blue it's raining, blue
faces of the lost sheep fading,
and I'm wading the fens with you—

you, in your wool sweater red as a robe
painted on a medieval Madonna or a king,
you, telling me about a new pigment
its blue born of crucible and accident,
you, my Sunday morning nebula
whose light has traveled so long to reach
me, overexposed in the rebel dark.

LETTER TO THE WOMAN WEIGHING LEMONS
AT THE GROCERY STORE

Last night you dreamed you could drink up all the air
        between the maple branches and moonshine.

It tasted of hemlock tips, resinous furring,
        sour and then bitter as the green underside

of sea ice approaching a country made
        of narrow rain.

Who will smell the twist of oil behind your ear,
        who will sigh against your morning?

POPPIES

Murmuring as with consent,
And gleaming as though alight
With a million, with a million
Loops and tassels of scent.
—SYLVIA TOWNSEND WARNER, from
"The Virgin and the Scales"

If I promise not to describe
the moon, will you come with me
a ways further into the night?
We'll wash the forest floor
of ash and find a fairy ring
half-eaten, muted crescent
bereft of power. We'll keep
our distance, braid rocks
to cross the low river, spent,
murmuring as with consent.

Maybe you'll recognize the place.
You were someone else, that morning
you gazed up at the lighthouse
growing from the mountainside.
Even afraid, you wanted to climb
beyond the spiral of ammonite
slashing your lungs. This time
take my shadow. We'll sweep
up each crest iced with pyrite
and gleaming as though alight.

We'll lie at the bend in the chasm,
panting. Below us the minefield
will sparkle its druzy teeth

as acres of ears chatter.
If you are cold, uncoil,
huddle against my vermilion
fever. You wanted to taste
oceans again. Further in, I swear
there's a garden, a pavilion
with a million, with a million—

We're almost home. Let
your blade go cold and smiling.
Listen: nothing binds us,
neither ring nor rope nor word—
I promised you a moon
without a single ornament
so nothing here can hold you—
not the dark, not even, my love,
the onyx poppies, their iridescent
loops and tassels of scent.

After days of white-green corn and soy, we turn north. Here the roadcuts are fresh, their striations pocked with small holes. You explain that new outcrops attract paleomagnetists with their coring drills the way a herring shoal's silver shine lures gannets from their roosts.

We are hungry, but still you stop. In the dust you draw the earth bisected by the neat cupolas of the geomagnetic field, then cover it with your open hand. Close it. When you lift your palm, the circle is barely visible under a fractured orchid. *While it's happening,* you say. You sweep the twinned arcs into place again. *After.* It's hard to tell what's changed.

Would you be able to feel it, the moment of reversal? I ask. Would your body know?

The process takes thousands of years.

A wren darts into one of the holes, a bit of parched grass in its beak. Not an answer, either.

*

At one point it becomes difficult to tell if the road will pass through the field, or if the field will pass through the road.

I had been telling a story of coming upon a field where no armies massed, no widows gathered. Silent and uncreatured, though the grass had been felled by a presence. In this field grew a tree, a pine I'd never studied, its interlaced branches a crooked net for light. And yet I knew it was the light, undirected and alive, that pulled the space between branches open. It could just as easily pull the space apart, and I feared that rending, as I feared the cloud descending over the sky, compressing it, a riverous rosegold disk expanding and churning toward the horizon, where invisible falls summoned. From the field, where the grasses dipped down into a dark hollow, I too felt a calling. Every kind of knowing ceased. It was as if each electric charge between us—the tree, the two skies, the light, the field, the water, my body—had aligned in a perfect balance of repulsion and attraction. Change, difference, information itself: obliterated.

I don't know how we are released, or when.

*

Far off, beyond even the vantage point where highways become uneven furrows of dust, we are two figures kneeling in a glacier's wake. You unearth some millions of years, I record field notes with my last pencil. Lost gannets, too far inland. Bark stripped from pines. The silver smell of water is a pressure low in my skull.

Tell me about the hollow, you say.

What force pulls the answer from me? The sky is a red plum, tart on my tongue.

An invitation. A mirror, curved around a core of time.

Neither of us feels the compass needle fraying.

In another life I'm a lamplighter, silhouette-reader, watchword-giver
        bound soon for my rest,
and you're the bridge-builder new in town, hitching hired horses to the dray
        while I unharness the light.

My shoulders ache. Now the harvest's in, more and more of the hours are given me,
        companion faithful as a spaniel,
to attend on the dark, to shape with flame its bounds and secret precincts
        where poplars sigh like the dead.

But I feel some change coming, a presence like a midwinter fever brooding
        in the eaves, a lurking
kind of appetite only consumption can dispel—. Babble this might seem to you,
        you of working day's domain

with your trusses and transits, your queenposts and camber beams, your strapping lads
        and strange commands—
molasses to hold a plumb bob true? A jest, I thought; but on a profile straight as yours
        where could whimsy roost?

If I appear to speak askew, remember I learned to veer and spar from fire
        splitting itself in pieces
and shadows snatching them back. Listen, I knew a woman who wanted doubly,
        silk slip of a second skin

and then sure as a storm she wracked our ferryman. So now you've come
        to span our sickly river
before it swells, you've come to find a way to bear our crossings' weight.
        I've noted you, of an evening,

watched you sway by the minister's hearth, drawing splinters from your palm.
      Enough to build a house.
What's it like to craft a solid, honest thing, a thing people know they'll use?
      You could tell me, of an evening

while we collect spent candles, carrying my ladder between us.   Quick now.
      The watchword's _____.
Dusk comes sooner than you think. Already you unhitch the tired horses,
      and I set out to harness the night.

COMING BACK FROM THE WEDDING

All the animals living, for once,
motion against the purpling trees,
dashing the way we came. Like guests
detained unavoidably, so very late
but who believe the dancing goes on,
the coffee's still hot, they belong.
First sleek fox, then dog-sized raccoon,
then possum, its eyes on us bright moths.
Last, when we thought our luck was over,
a bat's soft wings grazed the windshield
as if to say, won't you come back with us
don't you want to come back with us
don't you need more of this joy, unlooked-for
pillow on the hard bed of these days.

LOVE POEM IN HIGH HUMIDITY

Morning, breathless-hot
      your steps rainfall watering
tomato blossoms.

MERCY

Little Foxes

All that summer we played Mercy. We tried other games, at first: gathering red
pine cones as small as fingernail clippings into mounds large enough to bury
ourselves in, or coaxing each other to eat spoonfuls of the sand that collected
around the circumference of the cul-de-sac, blown in from a beach none of
us had ever seen and most of us didn't believe in. But it was Mercy we loved.
We grappled in the grass, twisted and squirmed like the neon fish ribboning
the river overhead. It was a good game, a fair game, since even if you weren't
the strongest you could still win by tolerating the pain without screaming.
How ferocious we were, how wily. At night our wrists ached. Our fingers
lengthened, pulled from their roots. We learned to read each other's faces, to
know how much effort a nonchalant expression required, what it meant when
someone gazed across the clearing, toward the water unspooling through the
birch branches. There was language, too, in the secret swipe of a thumb, the
angle of a braced thigh. Our lips turned plump and dark from biting. If our
parents saw the game from the windows, they must have told themselves we
were learning a complicated dance, stiff arms and mirror images. Anyway,
we were quiet, and we didn't need them. Relief. We splinted our own broken
fingers.

Cellar

That summer a preacher, or maybe a scientist, made camp in the woods on the other side of the clearing, then walked among us, singing what she claimed was the truth: the river ran from our mountains and kept going, going, all the way to the sea. She'd seen it twist and hurtle upside down, said at its mouth you jumped in, not up. She drew pictures in the sand, but the wind erased them, or we did when we locked our bodies to play. This was also the summer of the falling tent caterpillars. I hated their weight in my hair, the sparkle of their tiny barbs that gave me alone a rash. I squished them, as many as I could find, under my turquoise jelly sandals, and then tossed them up into the river to rinse off the treads—after the great rains the water hung low, almost reaching the ground in some places. I didn't mind squelching home. The parents wanted to burn the caterpillar nests but didn't want to offend the trees by their action or inaction. At night birds and bats came to feast, rending half the tents we could see to pieces. But it wasn't enough. The caterpillars kept falling until one afternoon all the ground we could see was a seething mat. We were withdrawn indoors. Left to listen, denned, while the parents spoke of prayer. When the tornado siren blared we played marbles in our basements, watching the dragon eyes whirl and roll on the uneven floor. They collected along the seams of other trapdoors. In the tunnels we could identify each other by touch alone: the wells in our palms, calluses from rings, the shape of the nails we remembered digging into the backs of our hands. Who took the preacher in I don't know.

Tether

We two were the best at Mercy, you because you liked to withstand pain, I because I was strong enough to inflict it. Sometimes at night, as bats winged along the river looking for caterpillars that had survived the tornado, we would climb down through the tunnels and meet in the clearing to play. You brought wintergreen candies. In the dark I could taste them whenever you exhaled slowly, pretending I wasn't hurting you. When you won you cracked them with your teeth to celebrate. The sparks they made lit up the glimmer-glisten of your wet mouth. One morning you helped me ice the tendons in my wrist. Yours was still broken. You said, or I did, *Maybe the scientist was right, maybe the riverbed really is a bridge from the mountains to the sea.* And the cool reply: *But who would cross it to know?* So it was your idea, or mine, but we decided. We braided rope ladders out of something I can't remember—in those days every house was a museum of attachments. We waited for the burnt orange hour to pass, for night, before we started. When we finally got a good look at the riverbed's layers cutting through the sky, I heard you crunching in triumph, and tasted mint. We threw a ladder into a birch and climbed to where the rock began, then kept climbing, up and up, one hand each. I bit my lip until it bled. At dawn we were a chain of two links on top of the river. We have been walking ever since.

DEVONIAN

In another life I am a fossil slick of agate,
once honeycomb coral, clustered. Crushed
in pressure's fist, I ache for your chisel's kiss,
I crave the sting of your hog-bristle brush.

In the sunrise house walking on stilts, the snake-filled water rises. It's Sunday morning. I am old, very old, my joints as conspicuous among my limbs as the lead strips between stained glass. I've lost my glasses. It's not my house, but the house of a friend. You are not so concerned about what kind of friend he is to me because you are fixated on the snakes. They are not venomous, not large, not hungry, and though I have lost my glasses I can see the lovely bands of red and black and gold roiling through the water that slips up against the breakfront, the wicker rocker, the pine sides of the bookshelf. I am still afraid, you know. I've lost my glasses. We have been here a long time, well supplied, because no one is coming to save us. No one can catch a house on stilts. The air rushing through the windows is warm, the water—more alive than water ought to be—is cool, like a washcloth on your forehead in the feverous night. I've lost my glasses and of course we should not be in love and there's nowhere we should be but here, this Sunday morning in the sunrise house.

DE PROFUNDIS

In another life I'm a vampire biographer
of many names, but these are the final days
of the Anthropocene, so nobody cares.

Human and otherwise, we fled our citadels
for caves long ago. I watched your mother feed
you a rabbit roasted over my gilt-edged books,

I knew her dreams of mute forests on fire.
I've been writing your life in bat bones, deep
in caverns too ammonia-rich for human breath.

You are Earth's last painter, old enough to render
from memory pelicans and foxes, strawberries,
hybrid daylilies I never saw open. I think you

must have loved light, must have loved what gold
was left of the world. No hair for brushes, you paint
with your fingers in the dark, with your own blood

you trace landscapes soon erased by cave-wall wet.
I suspect a temporary madness, this futile wish
I harbor, that you would paint my likeness too

for I am only a shadow, a long time hungry.
Besides, tonight when you ventured up and out
to glimpse the stars no ship could reach, I knew

you wouldn't return. I've seen that look before:
Paris, 1348, a goldsmith with your blunt nose
and strange heartbeat, river unsure of its course.

For months I watched her fashion an exquisite
miniature fountain, finer even than the sunburst
monstrance lifted for the new cathedral's faithful.

From an eight-pointed star she grew the stems
of fluted columns, bloomed shields and trefoils.
While her sister worked the basse-taille—for flowers,

fur, amber sun: copper in the crushed glass—
she raised crenellations and little gargoyles
to spout bergamot-scented water. I gulped

her midsummer sigh when the toothed wheels
finally flew and set the bells to ringing. (A song
their father, when he presented it to the prince,

called his own.) This machine, work of her hands,
would it stir you? Would you bend to drink
from the beaten silver basin, starlight on snow?

Or would you find it—beautiful and useless,
enduring centuries beyond its maker—repulsive?
But I digress. Soon after, the goldsmith melted

into a pilgrim convoy. Patient, I followed.
One crushed-rose night, the others sleeping
in a convent garden, she found, or sought

me, humming in a field of flax. Ready to be her rest.
How toothsome she was! And yet unsatisfying
somehow, to turn her face from mine, to leave

of her no trace. Penitent, with her rowan staff
I began to write the savor of her name
into the earth. A kind of life— ah, there I'll stay.

Out of the depths the bells call us to an unknown hour.
O my lady who's all along sensed my watching,
soon I attend you! Daylight beckons, last palace

of the chosen. On shores of ice you wait.
Breathless, I climb, I find—O my lady of nights
ever-fallen—the portrait you've left for me to taste.

IN THE DISTANCE

Archers, too young, light and notch new arrows in the distance.
Blameless, what symphonies might they compose in the distance?

Consider: surrender. A kind of holiness, brittle
drawbridge downed, calling out for fellows in the distance.

Economies of scaled creatures, marginal return of
foundering migrations—the earth we chose in the distance.

Grant me this, that until my end I may read and understand.
How bleak the text, how gilded the ginkgoes in the distance.

Illustrious lichen, sea light set in a wood: come back,
jacket with stars again oaks that once rose in the distance.

Kaleidoscopes, you claim, *will litter the edge of the world.*
Laundry, I counter. *Heat-scorched, it billows in the distance.*

Malachite the trees, topaz the broken sky: praise the farm.
Numinous the farmer, the soft furrows in the distance.

Over the ridge, flame tips the wheat with silky golds and reds,
plague at its heels, and storm. Famine echoes in the distance.

Quick is alive, a woman sighs, *rosemary, remembrance.*
Rivering, riverful—her breath shallows in the distance.

Silence filling with more silence: the bats hunting near dawn.
Tell me I'd miss the cobalt barn swallows in the distance.

Unless spiders weave, houses fall to flies. On every road
vultures wait to feast. A minotaur bellows in the distance.

We meet alone in hidden archives, re-carving ancient
xylographs. Time comes first; desire follows in the distance.

Yes, let gaunt care roll in, radiating its lunar chill.
Zaftig, we'll swell, eclipsing our sorrows in the distance.

NIGHT FLIGHT

Have
you
ever
seen giants—
lakes of land between
rivers—glittering? Seen them cast
a nimbus into the night, each life a light pricked out
by the cold angel of forgetting who darks the stars?
Morning, bare problem, advances.
Come down: the angel
awaits. Wants
to sting
you
too.

THE ALCESTIS MACHINE

Then / Nocturne

The town is dusty, all wrong turns and broken signs, the kind of place weather forgets to visit. Impossible to tell if you have arrived in the hour just before dawn or the hour just after dusk. The moon oscillates from wax to wane, wane to wax. A lake of fields—glimmers of wheat, flax, maize, lavender convince you, then disappear—laps against the road, pulsing in rhythm with an engine's tidal rumble. When you come to the proper house, you find it presses uncomfortably close to its neighbors, as if holding its breath for a family photo. All the windows are open. Fire could play hopscotch from one kitchen stove to the next. As you approach, you imagine a child whispering a dream of owl-faced horses to her friend across a narrow, deep divide.

Remember, the comma tells you when to breathe

An arrow and "machine around back" in hasty script taped over the doorbell, then your shoulders and chest scrape against stone. The descent is soft, easy, slow—*shillyshally, dillydally, settle down*—

You reach for the singer, stumble. Under the cold stream your feet waver. Lost coins.

A chemical glow pulls you forward. Strands of yew arils dusted with yarrow pollen sweep against your cheek, your neck. Hundreds of the bauble-bright helixes hang like stalactites from the ceiling, their rustle the telltale swish of a bead curtain in a half-remembered noir.

(Angel should quiet them. Is she missing?)

You mean to ask the figure sleeping—no, not sleeping; your notions of the strange have carried you too far—the figure concentrating, flicking a rope to life, braid of onions and chiles, goldenrod and Queen Anne's lace.

(If the figure has a face, she makes sure you'll forget it.)

The pressure in your ears now intimate as touch.

Unspooling film

Your end of the rope crosses you to a middle distance, to a wall of backwards mirrors. Projected on the wall, in mimeographed periwinkle-purple, the language of contract[1] and expansion[2].

Smell of silt, black as a grackle's breast. Electrons stilled in their cloudbanks. If there was a sun once, you've lost its heat on your skin.

In Silence—not the absence of sound once heard, but the place where there is not and has never been sound—you examine your missing fear. You admit the possibility of the machine's existence. You have known it all along.

To signify acceptance of these terms your signature is not required. Comes an hour your hands don't recognize you.

---

[1] *Terms and Conditions*
You may give only one day to only one recipient per appointment.
There are no exceptions and no refunds.
Subsequent appointments are not guaranteed.

Warning
Revelation of the machine's existence is strictly prohibited. Noncompliance will result in forfeiture.

Contraindications
Time travel.

Disclaimer
Not for use by children or the desperate.

[2] *Frequently Asked Questions*

Is this a dream?
Do you want it to be?

Can the machine raise the dead?
Have you unfletched the arrow of time?

Are anonymous gifts accepted?
Can you know whose borrowed time you're living on?

Will it be painful?
Yes.

Chorus

BASS: Should you afterward find your child gravely ill, or your mother, or your dearest friend, you may not return

BARITONE: in time. Should you afterward find your lover gone to some other, you may beg for your day back, but you will

TENOR: never receive it. Consider what pleasures, what insights, what encounters, you might

CONTRALTO: miss. Consider the length of a day, how the hours might be filled for the one to whom you

MEZZO: give them. Suffering, terrible to behold, has not been

SOPRANO: unknown. Consider that you may be giving away your own final day,

: you may be living your last hour now. Knowing this,

: : you could name the current that pulled you here. Or you could name the other current, the stronger current.

: Behind you the stairs are swept, clean and thornless. It would be nothing to climb them, nothing to give yourself back to the world. The boat is waiting. You've heard its engine idling.

: : You've already decided, haven't you?

In the space below

To disentangle love from desperation, an act of creation is the necessary proof, as each instance of the machine self-destructs and must be made again.

You have sculpted it with egg-studded sand. You have ground its pigments from a cliff face. Seasoned it with salt and saffron. Danced it into structure with your silhouette. Folded it even as time is folded around you now in the shape of a cave or a forest.

From the water at your knees you rip a sheet of paper the size of a child's hands stretched overhead in sleep. The ropemaker glides out from the other side of the mirror, offers you a posy of pencils, quills, charcoals, is gone by the time you notice the familiar twang of soft wood giving in to your bite.

make the machine, name its workings.

«

ø

÷

¬

±

¤

&

•

`

=

»

[through the flames

hoofbeats on the riverbed,

talons plunging into deep snow,

a name]

If / Aubade

Angel, *I'm saying*, Angel, what have you done?

(I am the stranger scooping up time in my two hands,
I am testing its heft, I am taking it home to tear
into waterfall pieces, I am treating it with contempt
or reverence, I am roasting it over a blue-veined fire,
I am burying it beneath the last cedars, I am

waiting,   waiting,   waiting   .)

All right, Angel. All right. Enough chiding.

Let's get on out of this cellar,
let's go feel the heat of the sun.

MAST YEAR

In another life I'm a swineherd relearning the forest
in pannage season, shadowing the forager pigs
turned out into stands of chestnut and oak.
Just home from the wars   you find me
gathering acorns for one dog-bitten and slow,
near to farrowing. Easy this year, the fallen oaknuts
a shoreful of smooth pebbles you scoop into the bowl
of your shirt, the way my sister holds morning
eggs in her apron. I want to touch your new linen,
marrow-colored by your sweat. Later, I'll shiver
        in the gray kirtle I've worn and patched
since before you left, alone on a pallet of moss
listening through pig-grunt and brook-talk
for the sound of your step. For now, we tumble
our careless harvest before the penned sow,
then follow the furrowed loam   deep
into woods where light narrows, lichen-chilled,
and swine feast in the hollows between roots.
Here you ask for my news. What I would say:
Last spring I found the ramsons growing thick
in ground worst used, stamped and rootled hardest.
The bluebells were a river that smelled of mercy.
I followed a damselfly to a beech and there unburied
a woman   etched in glass of gold and blue
only to cover her glint with earth once more.
Instead I speak of what you are ready to believe:
how the midwife saved the priest again, this time
from the bloody flux. Two summers so hot and wet
apples grew large as last-pulled turnips, balanced
in baskets on our heads—until a sudden spiteful gale,
slop of red—the costermonger's widow sliced
from the bridge, drowned in half an ell of stream.
But when hasn't there been a year of   dying

and living. To pluck mushrooms for supper
I nudge aside a snuffling pig. With careful fingers
you score a field through its mizzle-blenched hide,
and then your steady hands sweep and dive to show
me your ship, caravel-swift, swerving butterfly
against galleons, their green wakes   peopled
with sea folk, sails snapping like ice-downed branches.
You say you missed bread, and in the next breath
you sketch a kingly fish bigger than a brace of sheep,
its skin not made of scales but crag and rock—
could I have dreamed a life quarried out of the sea?
In all my dreams I'm bone, cold.   Still you're spilling:
On deck a clerk taught you letters in salt water,
not so difficult, you claim, as herding, those first days
of pannage time (for you were a swineherd too, before
you turned soldier). Come sunset you'll teach me
with bark and burnt twigs, you say. But your eyes
seek   the tallest trees, find only backbones
for ships. I take up my horn to call the swine in.
I know you've kept the worst of it from me:
harrow and stench, bellow and slow   deaths,
the kindness of your dagger in the dark—
as I will keep from you the widow's children
haunting the rain like   starved foxes.
This is love, isn't it? Leaving holes in our stories
        as moths make lace from their hunger.

NOTES

Epigraph to part one: This line is taken from Marilyn Hacker's poem "Ghazal: Across the Street" from *Names* (2010), and is reproduced here by permission of W. W. Norton.

"Winter": Edna St. Vincent Millay's "Eel-grass" appears in *Second April* (1921).

"Space Age": The source of the story referred to in the poem's second section is *Star Trek IV: The Voyage Home* (1986), directed by Leonard Nimoy.

"Figure Swimming Alone": This poem is for H. C.

"The Baltimore Monet" responds to the 2019 exhibit *Monet's Waterloo Bridge: Vision and Process* at the Worcester Art Museum. This poem is for Katie De-Pasquale.

"Self-Portrait as Illumination": My thanks to Shilo McGriff for help with this title.

Epigraph to part two: from Shakespeare's Sonnet 53.

"Lux Hours": Italicized lines in this poem are drawn from the English translation of Magna Carta, Lincoln Castle's copy of which I viewed at Boston's Museum of Fine Arts in 2014. My thanks to Tania Marchant at Lincoln Castle for assistance, years later, in tracking down information on blue wool dosimeters.

"Poppies": Sylvia Townsend Warner's "The Virgin and the Scales" appears in *The Espalier* (1925).

"Coming Back from the Wedding" is for Heather Barrett and Resi Polixa.

"De Profundis": The miniature fountain in this poem (and on this book's cover) is modeled on a rare Gothic table fountain (artist unknown, France, c. 1320–40, gilt-silver and translucent enamels) in the collection of the Cleveland Museum of Art.

"Mast Year": For insights and anecdotes about women's labor in early modern England, I am grateful to the scholars of the project *Women's Work in Rural England, 1500–1700* and in particular to Mark Hailwood for his post "Did Women Work in Agriculture?" on the project's website.

ACKNOWLEDGMENTS

My sincerest gratitude to the editors of the publications in which these poems first appeared, sometimes in different versions and/or under different titles:

32 Poems: "Flowers for the Virgin"

Cutleaf: "Deep Learning," "Devonian," "Manifestation," and "Strange Attractor"

Decameron Writing Series: "Equilibrium" and "Memphis Facula: Shot List for Improvised Documentary"

Equinox: Poetry and Prose: "Coming Back from the Wedding"

The Fabulist: "The Woman with the Suitcase Full of Stars"

Foundry: "Walking Alone"

hex: "Glass Hours"

Limp Wrist: "The Builder"

Lost Balloon: "This Splenda Packet Advises Me, 'Be the ENERGY you want to Attract'"

Matter Monthly: "The Archaeoetymologist Recovers *Bliss* from the Riverbed"

Menagerie Magazine: "Space Age"

Miracle Monocle: "Mercy"

Moist Poetry Journal: "Letter to the woman weighing lemons at the grocery store"

New England Poetry Club's *2021 Prize-Winners' Anthology*: "Salt Marsh"

Ninth Letter: "In the Distance"

Ocean State Review: "Letter to the Apprentice Jeweler"

On the Seawall: "Winter"

Paperbark: "De Profundis"

Passages North: "The Alcestis Machine"

Pedestal Magazine: "Figure Swimming Alone"

phoebe: "Self-Portrait as Illumination"

Plume: "Blueshift"
Sepia: "Mast Year"
Shenandoah: "Frost Heaves"
Storm Cellar: "Nyctinasty"
Superstition Review: "Poppies"
TAB Journal: "Celestial Bodies" and "Lux Hours"
Twyckenham Notes: "The Baltimore Monet" and "Night Flight"
The Worcester Review: "Trajectories"
X-R-A-Y: "Sunrise House"

*

Overwhelmed by gratitude, I take the liberty of quoting *Twelfth Night*—

I can no other answer make but thanks, and thanks, and ever thanks, to:

you, gentle reader;

the team at Acre Books, especially Lisa Ampleman, Sean Cho A., Taylor Byas, Barbara Neely Bourgoyne, and Nicola Mason, for giving this book your time and attention, and for your efforts in bringing it to publication;

librarians, especially those of the Worcester Public Library;

independent booksellers, especially those at the Montague Bookmill, Newton-ville Books, and all of Worcester's independent bookstores;

Aaron Shapiro, Amy Stepsis, Audrey Klein, Bobbie Ogletree, Brian Woodrow, Charlie Green, Dean Lamsa, Elizabeth Bacon, Emily Mohn-Slate, Hannah New, James Kocik, Jenna Commito, Joe Aguilar, Joyce Fukami, Judy Ferrara, Julie Phillips Brown, Karen Van Cleve, Kate McIntyre, Kate Dennis Nye, Katie De-Pasquale, Linda Denstaedt, Lindsey Gilbert, Lisa Usani Phillips, M.A. Sinn-huber, Margaret Millette-Loomis, Mary Cotton, Matthew Olzmann, Michael Goodfellow, Missy Hendrick, Rebecca Foster, Shilo McGriff, Susan Roney-O'Brien, Therese Gleason Carr, Thomas Dennis Nye, Violeta Garcia-Mendoza, and Virginia Konchan—for friendship, encouragement, and countless kindnesses while this work was underway;

my family;

and the stars of my firmament, Benjamin and Horatio.